Br
4/02

Multiethnic
Teens
and Cultural
Identity

Other titles in the *Hot Issues* series

Multiethnic Teens and Cultural Identity

A Hot Issue

Bárbara C. Cruz

Enslow Publishers, Inc.

40 Industrial Road	PO Box 38
Box 398	Aldershot
Berkeley Heights, NJ 07922	Hants GU12 6BP
USA	UK

http://www.enslow.com

Library of Congress Cataloging-in-Publication Data

Cruz, Bárbara C.
  Multiethnic teens and cultural identity : a hot issue / Bárbara C.
Cruz.
    p. cm. — (Hot issues)
  Includes bibliographical references (p.   ) and index.
  Summary: Discusses the many issues facing teens of multiethnic
descent, including discrimination and the search for ethnic identity
in an unsympathetic culture.
  ISBN 0-7660-1201-8
    1. Racially mixed children—United States—Ethnic identity—
Juvenile literature. 2. Racially mixed children—United
States—Social conditions—Juvenile literature. 3. Teenagers—
United States—Social conditions—Juvenile literature. 4. United
States—Ethnic relations—Juvenile literature.
    [1. Racially mixed people.] I. Title. II. Title : Multi-ethnic teens
and cultural identity. III. Series.
E184.A1C78   1999
305.23—dc21   98-054400
                                                    CIP
                                                    AC

Printed in the United States of America

10 9 8 7 6 5 4 3 2 1

To Our Readers:
All Internet addresses in this book were active and appropriate when we
went to press. Any comments or suggestions can be sent by e-mail to
Comments@enslow.com or to the address on the back cover.

Illustration Credits: Anne Brown Collection/The Peabody
Institute, p. 30; AP/Wide World Photos, pp. 14, 16, 36, 40, 51;
Corbis Images Royalty Free, p. 3; © Corel Corporation, p. 10;
Díamar Interactive Corp., p. 53; Library of Congress, p. 25.

Cover Illustration: Corbis Images Royalty Free

Contents

Dedication

For Amanda Jacqueline Yelvington,
one of the beautiful rainbow children.

Acknowledgments

The author would like to thank:

Jennifer Marques-Patterson and Jennifer Groendal-Cobb, for their unparalleled research skills; Ursula White, for her computer wizardry and creativity; Nancy Grove, for her generous assistance and comments; Rachel Rogala, for her insightful sharing; and the anonymous reviewers, for their thorough comments and suggestions.

Chapter 1

A Growing Population

Fourteen-year-old Mahin Root was looking forward to enrolling at Page High School in Greensboro, North Carolina. As she filled out the school registration form, she left blank the question that asked for her race. Since Mahin's father is white and her mother is black, she felt she could not choose just one category, either "black" or "white."

School officials eventually allowed Mahin to enroll. However, the U.S. Department of Education required the school to give racial information on all its students. This is because federal funding is based on that data. School officials were told to pick a category for Mahin if she refused to select a category for herself. They were to make their decision using the "rule of reason" or "eyeball" test. This meant that school administrators would look at Mahin and decide what race she most looked like.

In Baltimore, Maryland, Julie Kershaw faced a similar problem. Public school officials asked Kershaw to choose either "black" or "white" on her biracial daughter's registration form. When Kershaw refused to select just one racial category

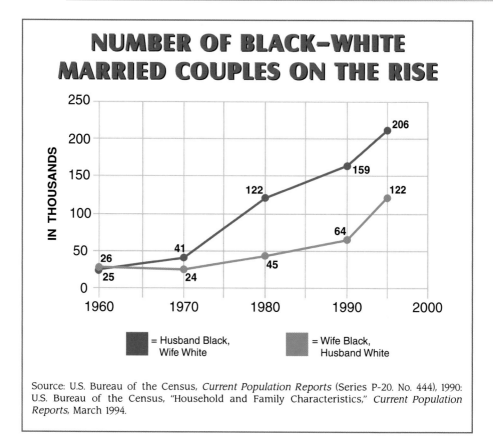

NUMBER OF BLACK–WHITE MARRIED COUPLES ON THE RISE

IN THOUSANDS

250
206
200
159
150
122
122
100
64
50
26
41
45
24
25
0

1960   1970   1980   1990   2000

= Husband Black, Wife White

= Wife Black, Husband White

Source: U.S. Bureau of the Census, *Current Population Reports* (Series P-20. No. 444), 1990: U.S. Bureau of the Census, "Household and Family Characteristics," *Current Population Reports*, March 1994.

for her daughter, school administrators said they would do it for her. Kershaw continued to challenge the system. At the same time, she considered sending her daughter and a foster daughter, who is also biracial, to a private school. Kershaw said, "If they [public schools] can't deal with their race, I'm a little concerned about how they will deal with them educationally."[1]

New Racial Groups

Across the United States, incidents like these show that the number of Americans who identify themselves as having more than one racial background is growing. This, and an increase in immigration, has been called the "browning of America."[2] These events also show how poorly the United States understands and accepts this growing population. A spokesperson for the Baltimore County public schools expressed his frustration at the current system: "We are required by the state to pick a racial code. [But] I think all of us are more aware that 'one-size-fits-all' doesn't work anymore."[3]

What Does "Race" Mean?

At the heart of the issue is the concept of race. The idea of racial classification is slowly undergoing a great change in the United States. For most of the nation's history, race has been seen as a biological fact that has been literally black or white. But because of immigration, an increase in mixed marriages and births from those unions, and a growing awareness of cultural diversity, America is beginning to rethink its view of race.

For most Americans, race is determined by skin color, hair texture, and the shape of a person's eyes, nose, and lips. This notion of race began to develop during the age of European exploration. C. Loring Brace, a professor at the University of Michigan, argues, "Race wasn't created until Christopher Columbus got across the ocean and said 'Good God, people [Native American population] don't look the same here.' It was really the settling of America that created that concept of race that we now have."[4]

In 1758, the Swedish scientist Carolus Linnaeus claimed that there were four human races: white (Europeans), red (Native Americans), yellow (Asians), and black (Africans). Linnaeus said that these were biological categories. He also linked

*I*n 1758, Swedish scientist Carl Linnaeus claimed that all human beings belonged to one of four races. He said these races were white, red, yellow, and black. Today, scientists disagree with Linnaeus and say that the concept of race was created by society, not nature.

each group with certain behaviors. For example, he claimed that Native Americans were ruled by custom and Africans were lazy and indifferent. He also said that Asians were naturally sad and greedy, and that Europeans were inventive and gentle.[5] This false and prejudiced classification system would continue to affect scientific thought for the next two centuries.

Today, most scientists do not agree with the idea that race is a biological category. Scholars have concluded that the concept of race was created by society, not nature. It is misleading to think of people in terms of "the black race," "the white race," "the red race," or "the yellow race." All humans are products of the mixing of peoples and cultures that has been going on for tens of thousands of years.

To show how useless it is to group people together into racial categories, anthropologists (people who study human beings) often use the example of skin color. Skin color is one of the main characteristics of racial classification. All human beings have pigment (coloring) in their skin. Some people have more, some have less. On average, blacks tend to be darker than whites. But a very large number of people who are classified as white have darker skin color than some people who are classified as black.[6] And while it is true that extremely dark skin is most commonly found in Africa, there are natives of southern India whose skin is as dark as, or darker than, many Africans. Yet the two populations are not closely related, either genetically or historically.[7]

Race is viewed differently through space and time. For example, French tennis star Yannick Noah's mother is French and his father is from Cameroon. He marvels that "in Africa I am white, and in France I am black."[8] And in South Africa, when apartheid was a legal system of racial segregation, the white spouse in a black–white marriage was legally reclassified as a black person as soon as the couple was married.

But just because scientists believe that the biological concept of race is false does not mean that they support doing away with the categories altogether. While race is a myth, racism continues to be a grim reality. Often, whites continue to hold the more privileged positions in United States society. Since many feel that we cannot ignore the discrimination against skin color that still exists, some would say that racial categories are still valid. We also continue to use these terms simply because we do not have any others on which we can agree.

The rate of married interracial couples has increased dramatically since 1970—by 275 percent.[9] The 1980s and 1990s witnessed a dramatic increase in not only black–white marriages, but Asian–white and Hispanic–white marriages as well. Additionally, 50 percent of all Jewish marriages are now intermarriages. This is an increase from just 6 percent in 1956.[10] Today, there are more than 1.5 million interracial married couples in the United States. These unions have created over 2 million children who are of mixed-race background. These people are no longer satisfied with having to choose only one category. They are challenging an outdated system and making their own place in American society.

Chapter 2

"What Are You?"

People of mixed heritage are often asked: "What *are* you?" One biracial woman said, "The mainstream is just curious. They will stare, and stare, and stare. Then they will approach you and ask, 'What are you?' Sometimes, it's no big deal. Other times, it's rude."[1] Rachel Rogala is a teenager whose father is African American and mother is Polish American. She usually answers the question by saying "multiracial" or "biracial." According to Rogala, "When I tell people this, some are pretty easy with it. Others aren't and usually proceed with the question 'What is *that?*' They want further explanation about my parents."[2]

Different terms are used depending on what people call themselves. For many people, "biracial" or "multiracial" refers to African, Asian, or American Indian heritage. "Bi" means two, "multi" means two or more. Others prefer "biethnic" or "multiethnic" when referring to cultural ancestries such as Hispanic, European, or Native Hawaiian origins. Many people simply use the term "mixed."

*F*rench tennis star Yannick Noah's mother is French and his father is from Cameroon. Noah says that in some countries he is viewed as white, and in other countries he is considered black.

Answering the question "What are you?" is often difficult because our society does not have many positive terms to describe this identity. Many people are also upset when they are forced to pick one race or ancestry over another. One multiracial woman recalls how as a child she used to wish she was just one race, so that she could have a simple answer for people who asked about her race. She explains, "I used to feel that if I just said I was black, then I was denying the Korean side. And then if I said that I was Korean, I was denying the other side. I just felt, why not embrace everything?"[3]

Forming an Identity

For most teenagers, adolescence is a time of fast growth—physically, mentally, emotionally, and socially. This period is marked by developing a sense of identity, self-esteem, and relationships with peers. Although teens may experience many wonderful new encounters and abilities during this period, it can also be painful as they try to make sense of the world and their place in it. In fact, researchers have found that between the ages of twelve and fourteen, stress for teens peaks dramatically.[4] For multiethnic or multiracial teenagers, this period is even more difficult if their identity is constantly being challenged or questioned. Added complications can include trying to successfully form one identity from two or more heritages and experiencing racism from two or more ethnic groups.

For many multiethnic or multiracial children, who they are racially is a source of confusion. In some cases, as children understand how racism is tied to one's ethnicity, children of color begin to show hostility toward their own ethnic identity. A significant number of them refuse to identify themselves as such.[5]

The biracial child may wonder whom to identify with. Blacks or whites? With her Asian heritage or her Latino ancestry? In United States society, these children usually do not have the option to choose all the groups that apply to them. Often, they select the group that reflects the ethnicity of the person who takes care of them, most often their mother. Children with one black parent and one white parent most often identify themselves as blacks. But this can be a problem because not identifying with

Tiger Woods
(1975–)

When Tiger Woods won the Masters Tournament in golf in April 1997, he was widely celebrated as the first African American to win the tournament. But Woods refused to accept the label of "black." He instead uses the term "Cablinasian" to describe his ethnicity: one-eighth Caucasian, one-quarter Black, one-eighth American Indian, one-quarter Thai, and one-quarter Chinese. "It's just who I am," he explains. Woods has said that he is proud of both his African-American father and his Thai mother and the support they have consistently offered. To identify with only one of his parents, he feels, is to deny the heritage of the other. He has said: "My parents have been behind me from the beginning. Their teachings assist me in almost every decision I make. They are my foundation."[1]

Eldrick "Tiger" Woods was born to Earl and Kultida Woods on December 30, 1975. Tiger recalls a rich and supportive family life. However, things were not always easy for the young Tiger. His family was the only interracial one in their all-white neighborhood. Older white kids once taunted Tiger and tied him to a tree.

When Woods won the Masters title in 1997, it was an achievement in several ways. His 12-stroke victory was a Masters record. It was also the largest winning margin in any of the four major golf tournaments since 1862. Woods had also set records by winning both the U.S. Amateur and Junior Amateur titles three years in a row.

Source: ¹Tiger Woods, "Foreword" in Earl Woods' *Training a Tiger* (NY: HarperCollins, 1997).

the other parent can lead to feelings of shame, loneliness, and depression. One young woman, the child of Persian and African-American parents, expresses her frustration: "Though some would suggest that being mixed makes me exotic or gives me the best of both worlds, I just find it maddening to never be fully accepted for what I am."[6]

Often, junior high or high school is the first time that biracial kids experience social problems.[7] Although they may have had strong friendships in elementary school, they may begin to be left out of social events or the popular groups at school. As teens become interested in dating, those teens who do not fit the "all-American" physical ideal may begin to experience anxiety and depression. This is especially true for girls, who may be more sensitive to the beauty ideals promoted by society. Psychologists also feel that children with white–Hispanic or white–Asian backgrounds fit into white society more easily than do children with one black parent.

Choosing Only One Group

Sometimes, when biracial children try to fit into one group from their mixed heritage, they are criticized by another group for trying "to pass." "Passing" usually refers to a person's trying to deny or hide certain racial or cultural aspects from his or her background to be accepted by some desired group. The person conceals his or her true identity. Thirteen-year-old Rachel Rogala, who considers herself biracial, has been accused of trying to pass. She says, "Black kids sometimes say, 'Look at her trying to act black!' But then white kids will say, 'Look at her trying to act white!' But that's stupid because what does 'acting black' mean? What does 'acting white' look like?"[8]

Passing usually refers to a person trying to join what that person thinks is the more powerful racial group. One example of this thinking is trying to "pass" as white. However, it can also refer to people trying to be accepted in minority communities by denying majority-race heritage. For example, some people try to reject their white culture and "pass" as African American. Karen Lucas-Brown, whose heritage includes African American, British, and American Indian, recalls trying to look more African American: "I would put bleach and Comet [cleanser] in my hair to try and make it kink up. I grew up listening to Nat King Cole, Chubby Checker, Smokey Robinson, Aretha Franklin—I wanted to belong."[9]

According to experts, passing may be a sign of healthy adjustment. These experts say that multiethnic and multiracial people have a strong claim to the richness of their heritage. It is up to them to select the culture with which they feel most comfortable. One teen feels that she has the right to "flow back and forth." College student Hayley Macon, whose parents are black and white, recognizes both cultures. She says, "It depends on who I'm with and where I am."[10]

Accepting Mixed Heritage

Despite the challenges that mixed-heritage individuals face, most enjoy the flexibility their backgrounds give them. One study of African-American–Japanese people found that when asked about the negative and positive aspects of being racially mixed, they made positive comments twice as often as they made negative comments.[11] A 1997 survey conducted by *Interrace* magazine found that Montclair, New Jersey, came as close to an "interracial haven" as any city in the United States. Other cities in the top five include San Jose, California; Denver, Colorado; San Diego, California; and Washington, D.C. One citizen of our nation's capital said, "At home in metropolitan Washington, D.C., our diversity has caused us no problem. Never have we been insulted or treated rudely because of our cross-cultural family."[12]

Ultimately, researchers have not found strong evidence that multiethnic people have lower self-esteem than people who consider themselves to be from one race or ethnic group. In fact, recent studies show that multiethnic young people do not have psychological problems because of their mixed background.[13] It seems that multiethnic and multiracial people are successful, self-confident, well-adjusted, and very comfortable with who they are. Seventeen-year-old Nicole Frierson, whose mother is white and father is African American, says: "My ancestors were going around conquering everybody. They were also the ones being conquered and, yeah, that's strange. But this is me, one hundred years later. I'm trying to conquer life right now."[14]

Chapter 3

The American Melting Pot?

People of mixed heritage have been citizens of the United States since the country's beginning. Joel Perlmann, a senior scholar at the Economics Institute of Bard College, insists that "American History would be unrecognizable without ethnic intermarriage."[1] Although immigrants to the United States have historically married within their own cultures, every generation that followed has been less likely to do so.

Interracial Marriage

The first interracial marriage recorded in American history took place between John Rolfe and Pocahontas in 1614. The first biracial Americans were the young people who grew up in Colonial Jamestown. They were the children of white–black, white–Indian, and black–Indian unions. At the time of the American Revolution, it is estimated that there were between sixty thousand and one hundred twenty thousand people of mixed black and white heritage in the colonies.[2] American patriot Patrick

Henry felt that intermarriage between whites and Indians should be encouraged and rewarded with tax breaks and cash awards.

But interracial unions were not accepted in all the colonies. In some cases, they were illegal. In 1662, Virginia passed the first law prohibiting interracial marriage. The state later passed a law that prohibited ministers from marrying racially mixed couples. The fine was ten thousand pounds of tobacco. In 1691, Virginia required that any white woman who gave birth to a mulatto child (having an African-American father) pay a fine or face servitude for five years for herself and thirty years for her child. In Maryland, a white woman who married a black slave had to serve her husband's owner for the rest of her married life.

These laws did not stop mixed-race births, however. During the age of slavery there were many mixed-race births. In most cases, it was because white slaveowners raped enslaved black women. As a result, there were enslaved people who were as light skinned as their plantation masters. White

Interracial Marriages

✓ 1970............... 310,000 mixed-race marriages

✓ 1980............... 613,000 mixed-race marriages

✓ 1990...............1,461,000 mixed-race marriages

Source: U.S. Bureau of the Census, *Current Population Reports* (Series P-20, No. 444), 1990; U.S. Bureau of the Census, "Household and Family Characteristics," *Current Population Reports*, March, 1994.

slaveowners are credited with inventing the "one drop rule." The one drop rule states that someone with even a distant black ancestor is considered black. This practice guaranteed that the children from these forced unions would remain slaves. Between 1850 and 1860, the mulatto slave population increased by 67 percent, while the black slave population increased by 20 percent.[3]

U.S. Census Categories

The first U.S. Census (population count) in 1790, supervised by Thomas Jefferson, placed people into one of three categories: free white male, free white female, and other persons (which included free blacks and slaves and "taxable Indians"). Seventy years later, the government began adding other categories like Mulatto, Chinese, and American Indian. The 1890 Census added further distinctions and had categories for White, Black, Mulatto, Quadroon, Octoroon, Chinese, Japanese, and Indian. Quadroon meant that one grandparent was black. Octoroon indicated that one great-grandparent was black.

These categories were questioned in 1896 when the U.S. Supreme Court was asked to review a case brought forth by Homer Plessy. Plessy, an octoroon, was not allowed a seat on an all-white train car. Despite the many racial categories that existed, anyone who was not "pure white" was discriminated against. Plessy felt that being seven-eighths white and legally defined as black was wrong. In *Plessy v. Ferguson*, the Court ruled against Plessy. It upheld the "one drop rule," and gave the now-famous "separate but equal" judgment. Just four years later, Booker T. Washington, the great African-American educator, said:

It is a fact that, if a person is known to have one percent of African blood in his veins, he ceases to be a white man. The ninety-nine percent of Caucasian blood does not weigh by the side of the one percent of African blood. The white blood counts for nothing. The person is a Negro every time.[4]

By 1910, the state of Virginia defined white as "having less than one-sixteenth Negro ancestry" (one black great-great-grandparent). In effect, someone with fifteen white ancestors and one black ancestor would be considered black. In practice, anyone with any known African ancestry was considered African American. The Census Bureau eliminated the terms *mulatto*, *quadroon*, and *octoroon*. It was assumed that three quarters of all blacks in the United States were racially mixed anyway. Anyone with any African-American ancestry would now be counted as black.

Increased immigration at the turn of the century brought much attention to the issue of race. The American melting pot was not as accepting as it is sometimes made out to be. The idea was to "Americanize" immigrants by having them lose as much of their unique ethnic identity as possible and adopt the mainstream white culture. In modern U.S. society, people of Irish, Italian, Polish, and English descent are usually considered white. However, in 1911 these four European nationalities were generally considered separate races.

Racism and Segregation

During the 1920s, there was a revival of racist groups like the Ku Klux Klan, whose membership grew dramatically. Intolerance of blacks was also shown in other ways. In 1924, Virginia passed a law that prohibited whites from marrying anyone with "a single drop of Negro blood."[5] Virginia was not unique; marriage between whites and blacks was illegal in thirty-eight states. Congress also passed the Immigration Act in that year. It contained strict anti-immigration laws limiting the number of "inferior" peoples from southern and eastern Europe entering the United States.

Also during the 1920s, African Americans enjoyed a period known as the Harlem Renaissance. During this time, African-American culture, literature, music, and art thrived. The movement was led by a group of successful African Americans made up, in large part, by mixed-race individuals. One of the outcomes of the Harlem Renaissance is that people who were considered nonwhite by mainstream society accepted identification as black. In effect, people of African ancestry began to accept the one drop rule. Many mulattoes began to identify with blacks rather than see themselves as a separate group.

During World War II, the notion of race was still so powerful that U.S. troops were divided according to race. Even blood banks were segregated according to the race of the donors. Despite unequal treatment, nearly one million African Americans served their country. They were among some of the most highly decorated service people during WWII. Many young people today are also surprised to learn that the "great American pastime" of baseball was segregated until 1947.

Although the one drop rule usually applies to people of African ancestry, during World War II it was used for the segregation of Japanese Americans. Special camps were created in the

Langston Hughes

(1902–1967)

Langston Hughes is often called the Poet Laureate of the Harlem Renaissance. During the 1920s and the early 1930s, African-American writers, musicians, painters, and intellectuals produced an impressive body of work. Using black dialect to depict African Americans' social reality, Hughes wrote plays, short stories, and novels. But he is probably best known for his poetry, resonating with the rhythms of jazz, which evolved as a musical genre during this time.

Langston Hughes was born in Joplin, Missouri, in 1902, although he grew up in Kansas. In his autobiography, *The Big Sea*, Hughes describes his mixed-race ancestry. Hughes' grandmother was of French and American Indian ancestry. He lived with her until he was thirteen, and they enjoyed a close relationship. Both of his paternal great-grandfathers were white. His maternal great-grandfather was also white and had several children with his mulatto housekeeper.

Several of Hughes's works reflect his mixed heritage. Although neither of his parents was white, Hughes was repeatedly drawn to the theme of a multiracial young man caught between white and black worlds.

Source: Arnold Rampersad, *The Life of Langston Hughes*, Volume I (NY: Oxford University Press, 1986), pp. 3-4.

United States to hold people of Japanese descent. The U.S. government feared that these citizens would support Japan during the war, rather than the United States. People with as little as one-sixteenth Japanese ancestry were sent to these camps. About one hundred twenty thousand men, women, and children were forced to sell their homes and possessions and move to internment camps. In 1988, the United States Congress apologized to the survivors of the camps and approved payments of $20,000 to each.

During the 1960s, the civil rights movement in the United States helped reverse many of the legal barriers against "race mixing." By 1967, sixteen states still had laws that made interracial marriages illegal. That year, the U.S. Supreme Court struck down the remaining laws with the case *Loving* v. *Commonwealth of Virginia*. The case was brought about by Perry Loving, a white man, and his African-American/American Indian wife, Mildred Jeter. Since interracial marriage was illegal in their home state of Virginia, the couple was married in the nation's capital, Washington, D.C. When they returned to Virginia, the newlyweds were arrested and put in jail for breaking the law. Police officers had barged into their bedroom before dawn one morning, shone a flashlight on them, and demanded to know what the couple was doing. Perry Loving had pointed to their framed marriage certificate on the wall, but the officers informed the couple that the Washington, D.C., license was not legal in Virginia.

After the trial, the judge gave the Lovings a choice: spend one year in jail or move out of Virginia. The couple grudgingly moved to nearby

Washington, D.C. They appealed their case, which eventually made its way to the U.S. Supreme Court. The Court found the laws against interracial marriage unconstitutional. Chief Justice Earl Warren wrote the Court's decision: "Under our Constitution, the freedom to marry or not marry a person of another race resides with the individual and cannot be infringed upon by the State."[6]

After the Vietnam War, thousands of "Amerasians" immigrated to the United States. They were the children that American soldiers had with Vietnamese women during the Vietnam War. Due to its long struggle for independence, Vietnam has a large number of mixed-heritage individuals with parents from China, France, and the United States, among other countries. Amerasians have had a difficult time being accepted in Vietnamese society. Black Amerasians have had the worst experience because their darker skin makes their mixed heritage more obvious. Faced with serious discrimination in Vietnam, these people sought a better life in America.

The United States passed the Amerasians Act in 1982 and the Homecoming Act in 1988. Although these laws were important first steps, they were far from perfect. It is still difficult for Amerasians to legally enter the United States. Once here, many Amerasians are disappointed to find that the United States is not the paradise of racial equality that they thought it would be. Especially discouraging for many Amerasians is not being accepted by the Vietnamese community in the United States. Kieu-Linh Caroline Valverde, an Amerasian scholar, feels that Amerasians are often seen as illegitimate. They are viewed as the products of illicit relationships between American soldiers and Vietnamese girls. Despite the difficulties in being refugees and multiracial, Amerasians are adapting and achieving in their new homeland.

By the 1980s, the United States began to experience a "biracial baby boom." Unfortunately, just because interracial marriages were now legal, it did not mean that interracial couples were well accepted throughout society. This point was made sadly evident by a Georgia church in 1996. The church leaders voted to remove the body of a mixed-race baby from the church's all-white cemetery. The decision made national headlines and public protest was swift. The church backed down and apologized to the family. It allowed the baby to stay in the family plot, buried next to her grandfather. Just one week later, the church drew national attention again when it refused to marry the baby's parents, a white woman and a black man. The case showed that strong racism can still be found in the United States.

As sociologist F. James Davis has pointed out, blacks in the United States have had a difficult time being accepted into mainstream society, regardless of the number of white ancestors they may have had. "Other racial minorities," Davis says, "can be absorbed if they become one-fourth or less of that ancestry. But most Americans do not even think to view blacks the same way as other immigrant groups."[7] As a result, people such as Martin Luther King, Jr., whose grandmother was Irish American and who also had American Indian ancestry, have been considered only black.

The U.S. government has a long history of determining people's heritage based on how much of their "blood" comes from specific ethnic or racial groups. This is particularly true in judging American Indian heritage. Many people believe that calculating percentages of "blood" to determine ethnic membership is absurd. They say that linking biology to cultural identity is meaningless.

The one thing certain about the concept of race in the United States is that it has continued to change. Asian Indians, for example, were considered Hindu from 1920 to 1940. From 1950 to 1970, they were considered white. Since 1970, they have been classified as Asian/Pacific Islander. In *Life on the Color Line*, author Gregory Williams recalls how a simple change in geography affected his identity. On a bus ride from Virginia to Indiana, he and his brother Mike were told by his father, "In Virginia, you were white boys. In Indiana, you're going to be colored boys. I want you to remember that you're the same today that you were yesterday. But people will treat you differently."[8] Williams was raised to believe he was white. When his parents' marriage ended in divorce and Williams's white mother left, Williams, along with his father and brother, moved to his father's native Indiana. There, his father's secret—that his family was black and not Italian as he had led the boys to believe—was revealed. Williams's story shows how the concept of race can change—from time to time and from place to place.

Growing Number of Mixed-Race People

By the 1990s, there were more people of mixed heritage being born in the United States than at any other time in the nation's history. In 1990, one in thirty-three children born was of mixed race. By

Anne Wiggins Brown

(1912–   )

Anne Wiggins Brown grew up in a strictly segregated America. She was born in 1912. The parents of Anne's mother were Scottish-Irish, black, and Cherokee; her father, a doctor, was the grandson of a slave. As a child, Anne loved to sing, and it soon became evident that she had a gifted voice.

When she was sixteen years old, she became the first African-American vocalist to be admitted to the Julliard School of Music. At the age of twenty-three, she was introduced to the world as an opera singer. She was soon chosen by the great composer George Gershwin to play Bess in the original production of *Porgy and Bess*. Because of her light skin, some people said she was not really black. But because she was African-American, she was not allowed to sing at the Metropolitan Opera, where only whites were allowed to perform. "I've lived a strange kind of life," she explains wryly. "Half black, half white, half isolated, half in the spotlight."

Frustrated by the lack of career opportunities because of her skin color, Wiggins left the United States in 1948 for Norway. "To put it bluntly," Wiggins says of her decision to move, "I was fed up with racial prejudice." She was welcomed in her adopted homeland, and quickly became a celebrity. Later, she became a teacher and a stage director.

In 1998, Wiggins, at the age of eighty-five, returned to the United States for a Gershwin Centennial celebration at the Library of Congress.

Source: Barry Singer, "Wings Clipped, She Soared Anyway," *St. Pete Times* (March 30, 1998), p. 5D.

1995, the number had grown to one in twenty. In California, one in every six births is a child of mixed race.[9]

As the United States reached the year 2000, it became clear that the census form would have to be changed to reflect the changing face of America. The last census, conducted in 1990, forced people to choose one of the following racial categories: White, Black, Asian/Pacific Islander, American Indian/Eskimo/Aleut, or Other. These classifications had been in use since 1970.

Many Americans felt that the selections available did not describe who they were. They opted to check off "Other" and use the write-in blank. On the 1990 Census, almost 10 million people marked their race as "Other." Most of these were Latinos who are unwilling to identify themselves as black or white. Americans using the write-in blank self-identified nearly three hundred races, six hundred American Indian tribes,

Adding Multiracial Category to U.S. Census

Question: Should the U.S. Census add a multiracial category so people are not forced to deny part of a family member's heritage by choosing a single racial category?

	Blacks	Whites
Add Category	49%	36%
Do Not Add	42%	51%

Question: Should the U.S. Census stop collecting information on race and ethnicity?

	Blacks	Whites
Should Stop	48%	47%
Should Not Stop	44%	41%

Source: Tom Morganthau, "What Color is Black?" Newsweek, February 13, 1995, p. 65.

seventy Hispanic groups, and seventy-five different combinations of multiracial ancestry.[10]

Some citizens started calling for an addition to the race category on the U.S. Census: "multiracial." In 1993, the Clinton administration ordered a study of the race and ethnicity categories. Under review was Directive 15, which controls the racial and ethnic categories on all federal forms. These categories are also found on school registration forms, job applications, and on applications for loans, mortgages, and scholarships.

Twelve-year-old Ryan Graham testified before Congress, explaining why he would like the option of a multiracial category. "I feel very sad," he said, "because I can't choose. I am *both*. Some forms include the term 'Other,' but that makes me feel like a freak or a space alien. I want a classification that describes exactly what I am."[11] Ryan's mother, Susan Graham, is the executive director of Project RACE (Reclassify All Children Equally). Graham supports her son and people like him, saying, "Right now, multiracial people are invisible and that's not acceptable."[12]

Graham, a white woman married to a black man, realized that the census form did not provide an accurate category for her children. When she called the Census Bureau for help, she was told that her children should select the race of their mother. But at her son's school, he was classified as black by his teacher based on his physical features. The bewildered mother exclaimed, "White on the U.S. Census, black at school, and multiracial at home!"[13]

But not all Americans feel that adding a multiracial or multiethnic category to the Census would be a good thing. Several African-American and

Race Question on Census 2000

What is Person 1's race? [Each person in household answers this question] Mark one or more races to indicate what this person considers himself/herself to be.

❑ White

❑ Black, African American, or Negro

❑ American Indian or Alaska Native *Print name of enrolled or principal tribe.*

_____

❑ Asian Indian

❑ Japanese

❑ Native Hawaiian

❑ Chinese

❑ Korean

❑ Guamanian or Chamorro

❑ Filipino

❑ Vietnamese

❑ Samoan

❑ Other Asian *Print race*

_____

❑ Other Pacific Islander *Print race*

_____

❑ Some other race *Print race*

_____

Source: U.S. Census Bureau, www.census.gov, 1999.

Hispanic groups, including the National Association for the Advancement of Colored People, the Urban League, and the National Council of La Raza, oppose a new category. They fear that it would decrease their numbers and dilute their political strength. They argue that the change would have a negative impact on minority voting districts and reduce the distribution of federal aid to minorities. Jesse Jackson called the multiracial category issue a "diversion" designed to hurt affirmative action.

In the end, after four years of heated debate, the controversy was settled. For the 2000 Census, the Census Bureau allowed people to check as many categories as they felt applied. Also, in an effort to make it easier for citizens to take part in the effort, Census 2000 used the shortest form since 1820.

Ohio Representative Thomas Sawyer, who chaired the hearings on which categories should be listed on Census 2000, said: "We are arguably the most extraordinary mixture of humanity ever gathered under one flag. It means that we are producing succeeding generations that blur those lines even within nuclear families."[14]

But while racial lines and categories may be blurring, multiracial and multiethnic people continue to face special challenges.

Chapter 4

Special Challenges

In 1994, a school prom stirred up racial hatred in Alabama. At the center of the controversy was a mixed-race teen and a white principal. In February, the principal at Randolph County High School called an assembly of seniors and juniors. The school's student body was 62 percent white and 38 percent black. Hulond Humphries, who had been principal of the school for twenty-five years, asked if anyone was planning to attend the prom with someone of a different race. When several students raised their hands, the principal threatened to cancel the prom. The junior class president, ReVonda Bowen, whose father is white and mother is black, asked the principal what his order meant for her. The principal allegedly replied that Bowen's parents had made a mistake and that he hoped to prevent others from doing the same.[1]

The community outcry was immediate. Although the next day the principal withdrew his threat of canceling the prom, parents organized demonstrations and called for a boycott of classes. About one fifth of the high school's students did not

*D*emonstrators gathered at the Randolph County Courthouse in Wedowee, Alabama, on July 1, 1997, to protest the swearing in of Hulond Humphries as the new school superintendent. As a high school principal in 1994, Humphries caused a racial uproar by threatening to cancel the prom because mixed-race couples planned to attend.

attend classes for several days. When the case came before the local school board, the principal was suspended with pay in a four-to-two vote. Bowen's parents filed a civil rights lawsuit against Humphries for the humiliating comments he made against their daughter. Even still, there were some white parents who applauded the principal's action and he was reinstated two weeks later.

The prom was held without any problems on April 23, 1994. About fifty couples attended under the watchful eyes of twenty police officers who were hired for the event. One of the couples was ReVonda Bowen and her white boyfriend. Just a few miles away, a "protest prom" was held by the National Association for the Advancement of Colored People and the Southern Christian Leadership Conference. Twenty couples attended the alternative dance, one of which was a mixed-race couple.

Eventually, the Randolph County School Board and ReVonda Bowen reached a financial settlement out of court. School officials admitted no wrongdoing but agreed to pay Bowen $25,000 for her college education. Then, just two weeks before school was to reopen in late August, the school was set on fire. Investigators found that it was the work of an arsonist. The fire further divided the community along racial lines. While many former white students had warm memories of attending the school, most blacks bitterly remembered the discrimination they had faced. Black protesters organized demonstrations and sang "We Shall Overcome." White supporters of Humphries arranged for a one hundred-car motorcade in the principal's behalf. Eventually, Humphries was reassigned to a new job, and a new white principal and black assistant principal were appointed.

The Randolph County High School case indicates how far the United States still has to go in terms of accepting interracial couples and their children. "I know that people are tolerating me, not accepting me," says one young woman, one of whose parents is African American and the other

American Indian.[2] Many multiracial and multiethnic people in the United States feel the same way.

Choosing One Group Over Another

One of the most difficult choices facing multiracial people is which ethnic group to identify with. Feelings of guilt and disloyalty can surface when a person is forced to choose one parent's ethnic group over the other's. A mechanical engineer who considers himself biracial says: "It's like having to choose which parent you want to belong to, and you love them both equally."[3] A past president of the Association of MultiEthnic Americans interprets the "check one box only" rule as a constant challenge to multiethnic children and adults. He believes that the forced choice requires the individual to answer the question: "Which parent and heritage shall be denied today?"

One parent may also feel threatened if the child becomes strongly interested in the other spouse's heritage. A biracial New York City teacher, whose mother is white, said that she would like to be able to acknowledge her black side without her mother feeling like she was being rejected. A young black Korean woman felt the tug of ethnic loyalties from her Korean mother when she cut her hair. "My mother looked at me with this really sad expression on her face," she recalls. "She said people would not be able to see the Asian in me, and that was hard for her. I didn't feel I was making some kind of statement, but my mother took it as a rejection of that cultural side of me."[4]

The feeling of being torn or divided between groups does not apply only to family members.

Multiethnic teens are often asked to choose sides at school. High school student Susana Jones, who is both Mexican and African American, remembers being asked to choose between those two groups by her peers. "One time there was going to be a fight at school between the blacks and the Mexicans," she recalls. "My closest friends were like, 'Susana, whose side are you going to be on?'"[5]

Another feeling that is common among multiracial people is the sense that they are the only ones who know how it feels to be of mixed heritage. Elliott Lewis, a television reporter in Orlando, Florida, feels that being multiracial is a unique experience that neither whites nor blacks can understand. Both of Lewis's parents are a mix of black and white. Expressing his frustration, Lewis says: "I'm too dark one minute and too light the next."[6] Biracial teens, for example, often feel that neither their parents nor their friends are able to

Newsweek Poll on Race Relations

Race relations in the United States are:	Blacks	Whites
Excellent	2%	1%
Good	10%	22%
Fair	45%	44%
Poor	41%	31%

Source: Sharon Begley, "Three Is Not Enough," Newsweek, February 13, 1995, p. 67.

Mariah Carey

(1970–)

Singer Mariah Carey has always proclaimed her multiracial identity although she has felt public pressure to choose whether she is black or white since early in her career. She complains that the press and the public seem obsessed with her racial background, saying, "I view myself as a human being. My father's Venezuelan and black, and my mother's Irish, and I consider myself to be a combination of all those things. To say I'm only [one or the other] would be negating the other things that I am."[1]

Carey was raised by her mother, Patricia, a trained opera singer. Her parents divorced when she was three. The stress of being an interracial couple in the 1960s and 1970s, the singer feels, put a strain on her parents' marriage. Carey recalls the racial hatred her family experienced: their dogs were poisoned, cars were vandalized, and she and her siblings were taunted. The singer acknowledges, "The thing about me is I always felt like an outsider. That's partly because I'm multiracial."[2]

Carey's vocal style is firmly rooted in black culture, which incorporates tight gospel harmonies. Her talent has been rewarded not just with best-selling albums (she is the 1990s best-selling female singer), but also with Grammy, American Music, and Soul Train Music Awards.

Sources: [1]As quoted in Christopher John Farley, "Pop's Princess Grows Up," *Time* (September 25, 1995), p. 75; [2]Lynn Norment, "Singer Talks About Her Storybook Marriage, Her Interracial Heritage, and Her Sudden Fame," *Ebony* (April, 1994), p. 54.

understand the special challenges that confront them every day. These troubles, some suggest, may make multiracial teens likely to experience depression, anxiety, and lower self-esteem.

Some biracial people feel as if they never quite fit into either culture. Michael Anderson, author of *Between Two Worlds: Searching for an Identity*, says, "I have suffered through my life because I am half black and half white. I have never been fully accepted as being either, from the black [or] white race."[7] One teen says, "I can't pass for white, and I can't pass for black. But I definitely feel there is a lot of pressure to align myself with one group or another."[8] For Lauri, the daughter of Japanese and white parents, it was frustrating to never be fully accepted by either group. Neither group, she feels, looks upon her as a member and instead associates her with the other group. She says that she usually feels more Asian with white people and more white with Asian people. One biracial college student writing about his frustration in bridging both cultures said, "My white friends want me to act one way—white. My African-American friends want me to act another—black. Pleasing them both is nearly impossible and leaves little room to be just me."[9]

The hardest time for biracial teens may be when they are not accepted by either of their ethnic groups. Adrian Piper remembers the taunting she endured as a light-skinned black child in her Harlem neighborhood. Black kids yanked her braids and called her "pale-face." Later, white children would call her racist names. Being made to feel that they are not "black enough," "white enough," or "whatever enough" is a common sentiment among people of mixed heritage.

Finding Other
Mixed-Race People

Some mixed-race children feel more comfortable in the company of other mixed-race children. One mother of multiracial children explained, "I've known other multiracial families, and our experiences are very similar. We want to protect them [the children] from any discomfort or confusion."[10] Rebekah Hopper, whose mother is white and father is black, recalls a painful childhood where she was constantly teased for being too light and told "to go stand in the sun to get darker." Now a twenty-year-old nursing student, Hopper feels less isolated since she joined a group called Mixed Initiative. The weekly meetings provide biracial students with a chance to talk about their special status. Hopper says that she looks forward to these gatherings because she feels completely comfortable there. Seeking out other multiethnic people is one suggestion provided by many psychologists who work with interracial families. One member of an interracial support and social group says, "We have really met some of the best friends of our whole life in this group. And, we've gotten really close with a lot of people. You are accepted no matter who you are or what you are. It doesn't matter to the people here. Everyone is welcome and everyone is loved."[11]

For multiracial girls, the pressure to meet American stereotypical notions of beauty—ideals that focus on white features—can be overwhelming. One German-Chinese young woman was teased and taunted about her looks. When she was in high school, she tried to look as white as possible, thinking that this would solve her problem. She lightened her hair, bleached her skin and gave herself freckles, and avoided the sunlight for fear of tanning. But rather than feeling happier about herself, she found that she was even more upset and self-conscious about her background. It was not until she started attending college, joined a multiracial group, and accepted her mixed heritage that she began to feel proud of her unique identity.

Sometimes, the beginning of the dating years is a multiracial person's first direct encounter with racism. Clinical psychologist Philip Spivey's father is black and his mother is white. He attended integrated schools and did not give his family's biracial background much thought. "It didn't hit me," he remembered, "until I was 13 and approached a white girl for a date. Then one of my black buddies pulled me aside and told me the facts of life."[12] Spivey's friends thought that a white girl might not date him because he was of a different race.

In the United States, marriages between blacks and whites are only minimally tolerated. This is largely because the social and political climate continues to be divided along racial lines. Yvette Walker Hollis, a white woman married to a black man, recalls feeling frustrated at not being able to find a mixed-race bride-and-groom ornament for her wedding cake. Her experience led her to create the magazine *New People* in 1990. Now the magazine sells a variety of multiracial merchandise, including wedding cake ornaments.

Despite the challenges, more and more couples in the United States are entering into interracial marriages. According to the U.S. Census Bureau, the number of interracial marriages almost doubled between 1980 and 1996 (from six hundred fifty thousand to more than 1.2 million). Black men are more likely to marry white women than the reverse, but overall, interracial marriages are increasing. The rate of white–Asian married couples has increased ten-fold. White–Asian pairs tend to consist of a white husband and an Asian wife. Most interracial marriages in the United States are between whites and Asians. One fourth of Hispanics are married to non-Hispanics, and one third of Asian Americans now marry outside their group.[13] President Clinton, at a town hall meeting on race relations, said that interracial marriages can "break down stereotypes and build bridges."[14] Polls indicate that acceptance of interracial marriages has steadily increased since the 1960s.

Despite the many challenges that multiethnic and multiracial people face, research shows that these individuals have an ability to adapt and be flexible. Some researchers propose that the special challenges faced by multiethnic or multiracial kids can actually make them stronger. But one issue still seems unresolved: the need for simple and positive terms to call this growing population of Americans.

Chapter 5

The Rainbow Generation

Until she gave birth to her daughter Addie, African-American Phyllis Ledbetter admits she never thought much about racial categories. Because both her family and her white husband's family enjoy a close relationship with Addie, they wanted a category for their daughter that recognized both sides. Among the possibilities they considered was to refer to Addie on government forms as "Anglo African-American." But the term is awkward and is not widely used. Ledbetter's family faces a common problem for mixed-heritage people.

Disagreement Over Terms

Although biracial and multiethnic people all agree that society should have terms that describe them, there is much disagreement over what terms to use. Some have proposed "biracial," "multiracial," or "interracial." "People of color" has been another suggestion. Others argue that "brown" is more descriptive; still others feel that words like "mixed," "blended," or "rainbow" are better. Here is how one person of mixed heritage thinks of herself:

I am multiracial—multicultural, even. My parents both are from mixed Black, White, and Native American families. I feel a part of each piece of my ancestral puzzle; this is reflected in my dress and my speech, both of which are as colorful as my ancestry. I don't feel a strong affiliation with *any* one race, so I "borrow" from all of them.[1]

Fourteen-year-old Sabrina Mathews prefers the term *multiracial* because, "If somebody asks what I am, I can't list them all. But if I say I'm multiracial, people get the idea."[2] Velina Hasu Houston is an award-winning playwright and cofounder of the AmerAsian League. She says that although her background is Japanese-American Indian–African American, she identifies herself as multiracial. Houston explains, "Politically I often call myself a multiracial person because I want to stress the political rights movement."[3]

Charles Stewart, Jr., who directs a support group for interracial families in Pennsylvania, believes that the term *biracial* best describes his own children. Stewart, who is black, and his wife, who is white, feel that *biracial* acknowledges both parents. Shaum Urquhart, whose parents are black and white, also prefers the term *biracial* since it recognizes both sides of her ancestry. "Now I can readily say 'Yes, I'm black, and yes, I'm white.' I feel I have the ability to identify either way and I *like* being biracial." When Chelsi Smith was crowned Miss USA she was asked how it felt to be the first black woman to wear the crown. She smiled and replied that she could not answer that question because she is neither black nor white but a blend of both.[4]

But not all people with mixed ancestry like the term *biracial*. One father in an interracial marriage explained, "Biracial just sounds too scientific—somehow inhuman." Some people prefer the term *mixed*. One mother described her anger at the limiting categories offered on the United States Census form: "I absolutely refused to put down 'black' as a category for the children. That would be denying their father. But they are not white, either. We have always said that the children are mixed." A Florida man recently sued to have his race changed on his birth certificate from black to mixed. Although the judge dismissed the suit, citing that it was beyond his authority, it has brought attention to the issue.[5]

Creating New Terms

Other mixed-heritage people choose to avoid traditional terms and come up with their own. One young woman, whose parents are Korean and Argentinian, calls herself "Korgentinian." Another young woman, whose father is white and whose mother is Thai, has settled on calling herself "Amerasian." This term, she feels, is "the best of both worlds." Other multiethnic young people have come up with terms like "China-Latina," "Latinegra," and "Blackanese."

Professional golfer Tiger Woods grew up calling himself Cablinasian—referring to his ancestry of Caucasian, Black, American Indian, Thai, and Chinese. Some African Americans were upset that Woods chose not to identify himself simply as African-American. On one radio station in Oakland, California, Woods was accused of undermining "black America, economically, socially, and politically." But Susan Graham, the executive director of Project RACE, found that accusation unfair. She said,

Bill of Rights for Racially-Mixed People

I have the right:

✓ not to justify my existence in this world

✓ not to keep the races separate within me

✓ not to be responsible for people's discomfort with my physical ambiguity

✓ not to justify my ethnic legitimacy

I have the right:

✓ to identify myself differently than strangers expect me to identify myself

✓ to identify myself differently than my brothers and sisters identify themselves

✓ to identify myself differently in different situations

I have the right:

✓ to create a vocabulary to communicate about being multiracial

✓ to change my identity over my lifetime—and more than once

✓ to have loyalties and identify with more than one group of people

✓ to freely choose whom I befriend and love

Source: Created by Maria Root, a professor of American ethnic studies and the daughter of a Filipina mother and a white father, the *Bill of Rights for Racially Mixed People* gives voice to many of the sentiments expressed by people of mixed heritage; Maria P. P. Root, *The Multiracial Experience: Racial Borders as the New Frontier* (Thousand Oaks, Calif.: Sage Publications, 1995).

"Instead of embracing him for what he is, people are trying to pull him apart."[6]

It is especially difficult to find acceptable terms for biracial people whose heritage consists of two or more minorities, for example, Black Vietnamese or Chinese Hispanic. Some of these people feel they do not need to choose a term at all. One young woman in a research study of multiracial people said, "When I was younger, I thought I had to choose between the Blacks or the Japanese. Now I realize that I can be both and who cares what other people think I should be."[7]

Many others, however, feel that it does not matter what special term one uses if the rest of society sees only one minority group. A student from a mixed family said, "At home I see my mom [who is white] and dad [who is black] and I'm part of both of them. But when I walk outside that door, it's like my mom doesn't exist. I'm just Black. Everybody treats me that way."[8] Hettie Jones, a white woman with biracial children, agrees. She argues that if society views biracial children as black, then families should raise them that way and not tell them that they are merely "half black."

Entertainer Bill Cosby agrees that, in our society, people with one black parent are automatically considered black. "If a white person marries a Chinese person," Cosby says, "the child comes out and it's Eurasian. If a black person marries a Japanese person, the child is a Black kid. We get the whole kid. We don't get half of it. Black people get the whole child."[9] Despite their interracial parentage, celebrities such as Halle Berry, Jasmine Guy, Lenny Kravitz, and Lisa Bonet have made it clear that they are African American. Actress Halle

Berry explains, "People say to me, 'You're just as much black as white.' I say, 'Look at me. When I walk out into the world, I'm seen as a black woman.' So that's the group of people I relate to."[10] Although Tiger Woods acknowledges both of his parents' backgrounds, the press continues to refer to him as a rising black star in the traditionally white sport of golf. Despite Woods's assertion that he is "Cablinasian," he is still considered by most of America as black.

Other people feel that creating new racial categories adds to the senselessness of race classification. These people want to end all ethnic and racial terms and categories. They argue that it is people's common humanity that should count. Francis Wardle, the director of the Center for the Study of Biracial Children, believes that, "The ultimate goal should be to do away with all racial categories because they are unscientific and therefore irrelevant, only serving to separate out people." Former House Speaker Newt Gingrich agreed, saying "Ultimately, our goal is to have one classification—American."[11]

But most people feel that that day is a long way off. Ramona Douglass, president of the Association of MultiEthnic Americans, says, "I'd love to get rid of the categories. But as long as we have them, I don't intend to be invisible."[12] Many groups have been created to support multiracial people. Founded in 1979, I-Pride (Interracial/Intercultural Pride) is the oldest multiracial, multicultural support group in the United States. Other groups have names like Interrace, Interracial Family Alliance, International Interracial Association, and the Association of MultiEthnic Americans. Some groups are dedicated

Halle Berry

(1969–)

Halle Berry has become one of the most popular actresses both on television and in the movies. However, Berry's childhood was not easy as the daughter of a black father and white mother. Her parents divorced when she was young, and she admits to confusion about her racial identity. She attended schools in both predominantly inner-city Cleveland and a largely white suburb in Ohio. Berry recalls a difficult childhood in which she and her sister Heidi were called "zebra" and taunted by white and black children alike. "When you're an interracial child," she says, "children can be cruel."[1] But Berry credits her mother with instilling a strong sense of self-esteem and a firm belief that the color of one's skin "has nothing to do with the wonderful person you are inside."[2]

Like some individuals with black-and-white ancestries, Berry has chosen African American as her identity. For her, she says, it is a political choice: "My opinion is that multiracial people do have to make a choice. Because even if you identify as 'interracial,' you're still going to be discriminated against as a person of color in this country. I think in order to seek acceptance from any group, first you have to accept yourself, decide who you are, what you're all about, and how you're going to live your life."[3]

Sources: [1]Laura Randolph, "Halle Berry: On Her Roles, Her Regrets, and Her Real-Life Nightmare," *Ebony* (November 15, 1997), p. 43; [2]Malissa Thompson, "Halle's comet," *McCall's* (March, 1996), p. 53; [3]Lisa Jones, "The Blacker the Berry," *Essence* (June, 1994), p. 61.

to specific mixed heritages such as the AmerAsian League, the Hapa Forum, and the Japanese American Citizens League. Many of these organizations publish materials, sponsor events, and hold regular meetings for interested people. Interrace even sponsors an annual "Interrace Cruise" for interracial families, couples, and single people.

In Hawaii, a state thought to be one of the most culturally diverse in the nation, *Hapa* is the term used for someone whose heritage is part Asian/Pacific Islander and part something else. It comes from the Hawaiian phrase *hapa haole*, meaning "half white." It was once considered a derogatory term but is now a source of pride among native Hawaiians. Similarly, the term *mestizo* (meaning "of mixed heritage") was once considered an insult in Mexico. However, the 1910 Mexican Revolution brought legitimacy to the term, and it is now respected by many Mexicans as an honorable symbol of national identity.

Susan Graham feels that people should be allowed to identify themselves. Because of Graham's tireless efforts, her home state of Georgia added the multiracial category to official forms. She recalls how excited her daughter Megan was when the category appeared on her school registration form. Megan said, "Mommy, there's my box!" Multiracial Rachel Rogala felt the same satisfaction when she took her school's achievement test this year. The preprinted form had Rachel listed as black. "So," says the thirteen-year-old, "I raised my hand and said that the category needed to be changed because I am *both* white and black. Because they had recently added a multiracial category, I was able to change it. It's great that the category is being added to official forms."[13]

Ending Stereotypes

Hopefully, the growing number of multiracial people will eventually bring about the end of stereotyping. Since multiethnic and multiracial people often understand two or more cultures, they can act as peacemakers between hostile groups. One writer, the child of a Japanese mother and African-American father, says that the offspring of interracial marriages have a very special role to play. "They, like me," she says, "despise the fighting among the different ethnic minority groups in America. They are able to act as bridges among groups, fostering communication and cooperation. The future of mixed people may be that of negotiators."[14] In fact, young people of mixed race have been called the best hope for the future of American race relations.

Even if there is no agreement on terms, one thing is certain: More and more Americans are beginning to consider and identify themselves as multiethnic or multiracial. Support groups for multiracial people have increased in number, as have student clubs on college campuses and Web sites and magazines devoted to the

*A*ll teens—regardless of their ethnic background—should feel proud of their identity and their heritage.

issue. Whereas in earlier generations people felt forced to choose only one category, many young people today assert their mixed heritage.[15] G. Reginald Daniel, a scholar of multiracial identity, has hope that this new generation will not only assert its own identity but will also do away with racism. "Multiracialism," he believes, "has the potential for undermining the very basis of racism, which is its categories."[16] As the lines between groups of people in the United States become more and more blurred, someday prejudice and racism may be eliminated altogether.

Organizations

Interracial Family & Social Alliance
P.O. Box 35109
Dallas, TX 75235-0109
(214) 559-6929
<http://home.flash.net/~mata9/ifsa.htm>

Multiracial Family Circle
P.O. Box 32414
Kansas City, MO 64171
(816) 353-8689
E-mail: MFCircle@aol.com

Multiracial Families Program
4100 – 28th Avenue South
Minneapolis, MN 55406
(612) 729-7397

Project RACE
1425 Market Blvd.
Suite 330-E6
Roswell, GA 30076
(770) 433-6076
FAX: (770) 640-7101
E-mail: projrace@aol.com
<http://www.projectrace.com>

Magazines

Child of Colors
P.O. Box 12048
Atlanta, GA 30355
(404) 350-7877
Magazine for interracial families.

Collàge
Interracial Family Circle
P.O. Box 53290
Washington, DC 20009
(301) 229-7326

Communiqué
Interracial Family Alliance
P.O. Box 16248
Houston, TX 77222
(713) 454-5018

Interracial Voice
P.O. Box 560185
College Point, NY 11356-0185
(212) 539-3872
E-mail: intvoice@webcom.com

Chapter 1. A Growing Population

1. Mary Maushard, "School Labels Difficult for Multiracial Children," *The Baltimore Sun*, August 5, 1997, p. 1B.

2. Richard Rodriguez, "The Browning of America," Pacific News Service, <http://www.minorities-jb.com/minorities/politics/archives/browning.html> (May 17, 2000).

3. Maushard, p. 1B.

4. Oralander Brand-Williams, "Census Change Stirs Mixed-Race Debate," *The Detroit News On-Line*, January 5, 1998, p. 2.

5. Audrey Smedley, *Race in North America: Origin and Evolution of a Worldview* (Boulder, Colo.: Westview Press, 1993, pp. 163–164.

6. Paul R. Spickard, *Mixed Blood: Intermarriage and Ethnic Identity in Twentieth-Century America* (Madison: University of Wisconsin Press, 1989), p. 17.

7. Carol R. Ember and Melvin Ember, *Anthropology*, 8th Ed. (Upper Saddle River, N.J.: Prentice Hall, 1996), p. 130.

8. Sharon Begley, "Three Is Not Enough," *Newsweek*, February 13, 1995, p. 68.

9. Daryl Strickland, "Interracial Generation: We Are Who We Are," *Seattle Times On-Line*, May 5, 1996, p. 2.

10. Joel Crohn, *Mixed Matches* (New York: Fawcett Columbine, 1995), p. 12.

Chapter 2. "What Are You?"

1. Rebecca King as quoted by Dawn Rohde, "Mixed Emotions: The 'Other' People," *Interrace*, September 30, 1996, p. 25.

2. Rachel Rogala, personal interview on June 22, 1998.

3. "Bi-Racial American Portraits," *WGBH/ Frontline On-Line*, 1996, p. 1.

4. R. D. Coddington, "The Significance of Life Events as Etiologic Factors in the Diseases of Children," *Journal of Psychosomatic Research*, Vol. 16 (1972), pp. 205–213.

5. Kenneth B. Clark and M. P. Clark, "The Development of Consciousness of Self and the Emergence of Racial Identification in Negro Preschool Children," *Journal of Social Psychology*, Vol. 10 (1939), pp. 591–599; J.D.R. Porter, *Black Child, White Child: The Development of Racial Attitudes* (Cambridge, Mass.: Harvard University Press, 1971).

6. Ziba Kashef, "Black, White, Other," *Essence*, August 1997, p. 52.

7. Jewelle Taylor Gibbs, "Identity and Marginality: Issues in the Treatment of Biracial Adolescents," *American Journal of Ortho-psychiatry*, Vol. 57 (1987), p. 269.

8. Rogala, 1998.

9. "Multiracial Americans Seek Acceptance as Numbers Grow," *The Sacramento Bee On-Line*, October 12, 1997, p. 5.

10. Oralander Brand-Williams, "U-M Group Gives Voice to Those Who Are Caught Between Racial Categories," *The Detroit News On-Line*, January 5, 1998, p. 2.

11. Christine C. Iijima Hall, "Please Choose One: Ethnic Identity Choices for Biracial Individuals" in M.P.P. Root, ed., *The Multiracial Experience* (Thousand Oaks, Calif.: Sage Publications, 1995), p. 263.

12. Della May, "That Is Your Child, Isn't It?" *Child of Colors*, June 30, 1996, p. 14.

13. Jean S. Phinney, "At the Interface of Cultures: Multiethnic/Multiracial High School and College Students," *The Journal of Social Psychology*, Spring 1996, p. 139.

14. Carmen Renee Thompson, "Skin Deep," *Seventeen,* May 1998, p. 193.

Chapter 3. The American Melting Pot?

1. Joel Perlmann, *"Multiracials," Racial Classification, and American Intermarriage—The Public's Interest* (New York: The Jerome Levy Economics Institute of Bard College, 1991), p. 5.

2. Lawrence Wright, "One Drop of Blood," *The New Yorker*, July 24, 1994, p. 6.

3. Naomi Zack, Race and Mixed Race (Philadelphia: Temple University Press, 1993), p. 82.

4. Booker T. Washington, *The Future of the American Negro* (Boston: Small, Maynard and Co., 1900), p. 158, as quoted in John G. Mencke, Mulattoes and Race Mixture (Ann Arbor: University of Michigan Institute of Research Press, 1979), p. 37.

5. Ellis Cose, "One Drop of Bloody History," *Newsweek*, February 13, 1995, p. 70.

6. *Loving* v. *Virginia* 388 U.S. (1967).

7. Cose, p. 70.

8. Gregory Howard Williams, *Life on the Color Line: The True Story of a White Boy Who Discovered He Was Black* (New York: Penguin Books, 1995), p. 33.

9. "Multiracial Americans Seek Acceptance as Numbers Grow," *The Sacramento Bee On-Line*, October 12, 1997, p. 2.

10. Tom Morganthau, "What Color Is Black?" *Newsweek*, February 13, 1995, p. 65.

11. Amy Laughinghouse, "Categoric Denials," *Creative Loafing*, June 14, 1997, p. 1.

12. Lynn Schnailberg, "U.S. Considers Adding Statistics on 'Multiracial,'" Education Week on the Web, June 25, 1997, p. 2.

13. As quoted by Dinesh D'Souza, "As I See It: The One-Drop-of-Blood Rule," *Forbes Today*, December 2, 1996.

14. Daryl Strickland, "Interracial Generation: We Are Who We Are," *Seattle Times On-Line*, May 5, 1996, p. 2.

Chapter 4. Special Challenges

1. Ronald Smothers, "U.S. Moves to Oust Principal in Furor on Interracial Dating," *The New York Times*, May 18, 1994, p. 20A.

2. Jill Smolowe, "Intermarried . . . with Children," *Time*, Fall 1993, p. 66.

3. Kook Dean as quoted in Itabari Njeri, "A Sense of Identity," *Los Angeles Times*, June 5, 1988, p. F1.

4. Fay Yarbrough as quoted by Jack E. White, "I'm Just Who I Am," *Time*, May 5, 1997, p. 34.

5. Carmen Renee Thompson, "Skin Deep," *Seventeen*, May 1998, p. 160.

6. Maria T. Padilla, "Shades of Difference," *The Orlando Sentinel*, May 7, 1997, p. E1.

7. Larry Dougherty, "Man Sues To Change Racial Designation," *St. Pete Times*, April 18, 1998, p. 3B.

8. Sheba Howerton as quoted in Jack E. White, "I'm Just Who I Am," *Time*, May 5, 1997, p. 34.

9. Brian A. Courtney, "Freedom from Choice: Being Biracial Has Meant Denying Half My Identity," *Newsweek*, February 13, 1995, p. 16.

10. Padilla, p. 1E.

11. Nancy Williams as quoted by Gabrielle Songe, "Biracial Unions Boom," *Tri-State Defender*, July 5, 1995, p. 1A.

12. Eileen Keerdoja, "Children of the Rainbow," *Newsweek*, November 19, 1984, p. 120.

13. Dinesh D'Souza, "As I See It: The One-Drop-of-Blood Rule," *Forbes Today*, December 2, 1996.

14. Tananarive Due, "Beyond Race," *The Miami Herald*, December 13, 1997, pp. 1G, 2G.

Chapter 5. The Rainbow Generation

1. Belinda Paschal, *Interrace*, January/February 1993, p. 202.

2. Maria T. Padilla, "Shades of Difference," *The Orlando Sentinel*, May 7, 1997, p. 1E.

3. Itabari Njeri, "Call for Census Category Creates Interracial Debate," *Los Angeles Times*, January 13, 1991, pp. 8E–9E.

4. Lynn Norment, "Am I Black, White, or In Between?" *Ebony*, August 1995, p. 112.

5. Larry Dougherty, "Man Sues to Change Racial Designation," *St. Pete Times*, April 18, 1998, p. 3B.

6. Padilla, p. 1E.

7. Christine C. Iijima Hall, "Please Choose One: Ethnic Identity Choices for Biracial Individuals," in M.P.P. Root, ed., *The Multiracial Experience* (Thousand Oaks, Calif.: Sage Publications, 1995), p. 256.

8. Paul R. Spickard, *Mixed Blood: Intermarriage and Ethnic Identity in Twentieth-Century America* (Madison: University of Wisconsin Press, 1989), p. 360.

9. Bill Cosby, *Bill Cosby: In Words and Pictures* (Chicago: Johnson Publishing Company, 1986), p. 167.

10. Johnny Dodd, "Portrait in Black and White," *People Weekly*, February 23, 1998, p. 19.

11. Jerelyn Eddings, "Counting a 'New' Type of American," *U.S. News On-Line*, July 14, 1997, p. 2.

12. Daryl Strickland, "Interracial Generation: We Are Who We Are," *Seattle Times On-Line*, May 5, 1996, p. 4.

13. Rachel Rogala, personal interview on June 22, 1998.

14. Hall, p. 329.

15. "Multiracial Americans Seek Acceptance as Numbers Grow," *The Sacramento Bee On-Line*, October 12, 1997, pp. 2–3.

16. Lawrence Wright, "One Drop of Blood," *The New Yorker*, July 24, 1994, p. 6.

Bender, David, and Bruno Leone, eds. *Interracial America: Opposing Viewpoints*. San Diego, Calif.: Greenhaven Press, 1996.

Crohn, Joel. *Mixed Matches*. New York: Fawcett Columbine, 1995.

Funderburg, Lise. *Black, White, Other: Biracial Americans Talk About Race and Identity*. New York: William Morrow and Company, 1994.

Gay, Kathlyn. *The Rainbow Effect: Interracial Families*. New York: Franklin Watts, 1987.

Gillespie, Peggy, and Gigi Kaeser. *Of Many Colors: Portraits of Multiracial Families*. Amherst: University of Massachusetts Press, 1997.

Nash, Renea D. *Coping as a Biracial/Biethnic Teen*. New York: Rosen Publishing Group, 1995.

Root, Maria P. P. *Racially Mixed People in America: Within, Between & Beyond Race*. Thousand Oaks, Calif.: Sage Publications, 1992.

Root, Maria P. P., ed. *The Multiracial Experience: Racial Borders as the New Frontier*. Thousand Oaks, Calif.: Sage Publications, 1995.

Zack, Naomi. *Race and Mixed Race*. Philadelphia: Temple University Press, 1993.

Further Reading